Tenderfella

by Michael Liebo

Baker's Plays
c/o Samuel French, Inc.
45 West 25 Street
New York, NY 10010
bakersplays.com

NOTICE

This book is offered for sale at the price quoted only on the understanding that, if any additional copies of the whole or any part are necessary for its production, such additional copies will be purchased. The attention of all purchasers is directed to the following: this work is fully protected under the copyright laws of the United States of America, the British Commonwealth, including Canada, and all other countries of the Copyright Union. Violations of the Copyright Law are punishable by fine or imprisonment, or both. The copying or duplication of this work or any part of this work, by hand or by any process, is an infringement of the copyright and will be vigorously prosecuted.

This play may not be produced by amateurs or professionals for public or private performance without first submitting application for performing rights. Licensing fees are due on all performances whether for charity or gain, or whether admission is charged or not. Since performance of this play without the payment of the licensing fee renders anybody participating liable to severe penalties imposed by the law, anybody acting in this play should be sure, before doing so, that the licensing fee has been paid. Professional rights, reading rights, radio broadcasting, television and all mechanical rights, etc. are strictly reserved. Application for performing rights should be made directly to BAKER'S PLAYS.

No one shall commit or authorize any act or omission by which the copyright of, or the right to copyright, this play may be impaired. No one shall make any changes in this play for the purpose of production.

Publication of this play does not imply availability for performance. Both amateurs and professionals considering a production are strongly advised in their own interest to apply to Baker's Plays for written permission before starting rehearsals, advertising, or booking a theatre.

Whenever the play is produced, the author's name must be carried in all publicity, advertising and programs. Also, the following notice must appear on all printed programs, "Produced by special arrangement with Baker's Plays."

Licensing fees for TENDERFELLA are based on a per performance rate and payable one week in advance of the production.

Please consult the Baker's Plays website at www.bakersplays.com or our current print catalogue for up to date licensing fee information.

TENDERFELLA
ISBN 978-0-87440-300-8
#1815-B

TENDERFELLA was presented at Judkins Middle School in May, 2007.

TENDERFELLA:	Cody Portwood
NARRATOR:	Mia McKinstry
JOSH:	Michael Day
ANNETTE:	Sophie McGuirk
CHEERLEADER 1:	Lisa Mitchell
CHEERLEADER 2:	Morgan Ward
CHEERLEADER 3:	Taylor Cella
CHEERLEADER 4:	Sharmaine Abuan
BYSTANDER:	Nikkol Mitchell
JENNY:	Taelor Janes
WILLARD:	Aaron Ley
COACH:	Hunter Norton
BILLY JEAN:	Emily Liebo
ARNOLD:	Josh Wells
DUKE:	Jordan Hawley
FLORENCE:	Katie Doi
BABE:	Alexa May
JOHNNY:	Cameron Chubb
MARK:	Nathan Fair
JENNIFER:	Alycia Duron
TOM:	Victor Spooner
JOHN:	Soren Richards
CRENSHAW:	Lindsay Zoff
ROXANNE:	Madison Murphy-Sinclair
DIRECTOR:	Rebecca Kovach
THEO:	Evan Lange
MR. JANICO:	Ashley Collins
AGENT:	Megan Cota
MAX:	Skyler Larson
PRODUCER:	Haley Dockstader
FAN:	Missy Siebert
BRENDA:	Vishwa Patel
AMANDA:	Nikkol Mitchell
DONNA:	Leanne Gregory
ALBERT:	Brody Crawford
GIRL 1:	Alex Manuele
GIRL 2:	Jesenya Magana
ANNOUNCER:	Brooke Coffman

CAST OF CHARACTERS

ROXANNE JANICO
NARRATOR
DIRECTOR
ANNETTE
THEO
JOSH
MRS. JANICO
CHEERLEADERS
AGENT
BYSTANDER
MAX
JENNY
PRODUCER
WILLARD
RADIO HOST
COACH
COACH'S WIFE
AUDIENCE MEMBER 1
AUDIENCE MEMBER 2
FOOTBALL TEAM
TENDERFELLA
BRENDA
BILLY JEAN
AMANDA
ARNOLD
DONNA
DUKE
ALBERT
FLORENCE
GIRL1
GIRL 2
BABE
JOHNNY
ANNOUNCER
MARK
VARIOUS JUDKINS STUDENTS
JENNIFER
TOM
JOHN
CRENSHAW

NARRATOR. At this very moment there are 6,562,677,453 people who inhabit earth. That means there are 6,562,677,453 stories that could be told tonight. The fact of the matter is that everyone is interesting; there just has to be someone who can put their stories into words. So tonight could have been a story about Annette. *(ANNETTE enters.)* She was on track to be the top seller in North America for Avon.

ANNETTE. *(To NARRATOR)* Hi, my name is Annette Bowen, and when I'm finished talking with you, your life will be changed. I can already see doubt in your face, but I kid you not, the answers you seek are in my briefcase. "What answers?" you ask. Good question. I am talking about your skin. No more acne. No more flakiness. No more discoloration. Your skin will be smooth and silky for the rest of your life. Your face will glow, your hair will shine, and your legs will be smoother than you could have ever imagined. I am a representative for Avon, and our goal is your beauty and happiness. Now, let me demonstrate what I have for you.

(She reaches into her briefcase as the NARRATOR continues.)

NARRATOR. Annette could have gone far if she hadn't have knocked on the wrong door. She tried to sell her skin care products to a ship full of pirates. Rather than buying anything, they kidnapped her and forced poor Annette to be a deck hand for the remainder of her life.

(Six pirates run in and carry ANNETTE off.)

ANNETTE. Hey, what are you guys doing? Put me down! Your hands are gross. By the way, Avon carries a skin cleanser that will cut right through that grease.

NARRATOR. Or our story tonight could be about Josh Colbert. Josh was destined to be one of the great photographers of all time.

(**JOSH** *comes out with six girls, dressed as cheerleaders.*)

JOSH. Okay ladies, work with me. Let's see a cheer pose. Excellent. Look as if your team has just scored a basket. That's right. Now your team is losing the game. Give me a worried look. Perfect. Let's see the flyer take flight. Hold her up. Good. Good. And let me get a close up here; okay, drop her.

(**JOSH** *lets out a scream as the flyer is dropped on him.*)

NARRATOR. Unfortunately for Mr. Colbert, the flyer was dropped accidentally on him, breaking both hands. He was never able to snap a picture again.

JOSH. I need a doctor! Get me a doctor!

CHEERLEADER. Jeez, Mr. Colbert, your hands look crooked.

(*They exit*)

NARRATOR. Or for that matter, our story could be about Jenny. She was just about to make it into the Guinness World Book of Records. She had been laughing for thirty-six hours straight. She only had twenty minutes left to go.

(**JENNY** *comes out laughing.*)

She would have made it, too, if someone hadn't asked her an innocent question.

BYSTANDER. Do you mind me asking, what's so funny?

(**JENNY** *stops laughing, realizes what she's done and exits screaming.*)

JENNY. What did you ask me that for? What did you ask me that for?

NARRATOR. Our choice for a story can go on and on. Even so, I think we've found the perfect plot. It's about a young man who seemingly doesn't have a lot to offer.

(TENDERFELLA comes out and starts to play solitaire.)

His real name is Rocky Ackerson. As you can see, he's involved in an intense round of solitaire. For the next forty minutes you'll get to know him by his nickname, Tenderfella. This is how he got that name. You'll notice next to Rocky are his friends, who happen to be ants. Rocky ordered an ant farm from Google and could watch his tiny, industrious pets for hours. Rocky loved his ants and took them wherever he went. Did you ever notice how when somebody is a bit, well, different, there always has to be a smart aleck who can't leave him alone? In this case, it was in the form of the school bully, Willard. Willard knew that every day Rocky played solitaire, with his ant friends watching. Willard pulled a rather mean stunt at Rocky's expense, not to mention the ants'.

(WILLARD, who has a group of friends around him, approaches ROCKY.)

WILLARD. Hey, Rocky, did you notice how our school has been invaded by bugs? Why look, you've got a bunch of them right next to you. Good thing I have some Raid in my backpack.

(WILLARD takes out his raid and kills the ants.)

NARRATOR. That's right, every last ant perished at the hands of Willard. Had he done that to my pets, I'd want to take him by the neck and throw him into a dungeon for the next thirty years.

(The narrator grabs WILLARD and throws him into a dungeon. WILLARD screams.)

WILLARD. Let me out of here! Let me out of here!

(The NARRATOR lets him out.)

Jeez Louise!

(WILLARD walks back to his friends.)

NARRATOR. But that's me. As it was, Willard continued to torment poor Rocky.

TENDERFELLA. You didn't need to do that, they didn't do anything to you.

WILLARD. Ah, little Rocky is upset. Boo hoo! Why don't you hit me, Rocky? I dare you, hit me!

NARRATOR. But Rocky didn't hit Willard. He didn't believe in violence. He just stared at his deceased friends and cried.

WILLARD. Look, the loser is crying. He's crying over dead ants. What a "tender fella." That's what Rocky is, a tender fella. Let's go or we're all likely to cry, too.

(Everyone leaves, pretending to cry.)

See ya, Tenderfella!

NARRATOR. And from there on the nickname stuck. Even Rocky's brothers and sisters started calling him Tenderfella. Oh, speaking of Tenderfella's family, I should spend a couple of minutes talking about them. His dad was called "Coach."

(A whistle is blown and **COACH** *comes out with a group of kids, running in place.)*

COACH. Get those knees up higher. Higher I say! Pick up your pace. Faster. Faster. Faster. Now give me some push-ups. Ready: one, two, three, four five, six, seven, eight, nine, and ten. All right, boys, here's my favorite, tossing the bowling ball. I don't want to see anyone drop it on your foot. Let's go, pass it, ladies.

(Bowling ball is passed around as the players grunt.)

NARRATOR. Coach Ackerson's dream was to be a professional football coach for the Green Bay Packers. That never happened. Then, he hoped to take over at Ohio State. That didn't happen either. His next goal was to be the coach where he'd played high school ball, Paxton High. No availability there, either. So he had to settle as coach of a Pop Warner football team.

COACH. If we're gonna make the playoffs, I'm going to need to see a bit more hustle. Let's take another ten mile jog. *(Begins to sing marine style.)* Who's the meanest in the town?

TEAM. *(running in place)* We're the meanest in the town.

COACH. Who's afraid when we're around?

TEAM. The world's afraid when we're around.

COACH. Sound off.

TEAM. One. Two.

COACH. Sound off.

TEAM. Three. Four. One, two. Three four.

> *(They all take off.* **COACH** *follows them singing.)*

COACH. Who's the toughest on the field?

TEAM. *(Off stage)* We're the toughest on the field.

NARRATOR. Coach and his wife had seven children: Babe, Arnold, Billy Jean, Duke, Florence, Johnny, and, of course, Rocky. *(As* **NARRATOR** *speaks,* **COACH'S WIFE** *enters pushing a baby stroller. She reacts to* **NARRATOR** *'s commentary.)* One day Coach's wife looked into the stroller and came to the realization she had enough children for a basketball team. She promptly took off running and never stopped. Coach took over all parental duties and raised some incredible athletes. Arnold, named after golf icon, Arnold Palmer, became one of the fiercest middle line backers in high school football. You'd think Arnold would've been a pro golfer, but, no... Coach didn't care what sport his kids played, as long as they had a famous sports figure's name, and played a game!

> *(A student is carrying a football and* **ARNOLD** *tackles him.)*

Babe, who was named after the legendary baseball player, Babe Ruth, was so quick in club soccer it always seemed that everyone was standing still whenever she scored a goal.

> *(Three soccer players are standing still as* **BABE** *weaves past them before she kicks the ball.)*

Duke, named after the father of surfing, Duke Kahanamoku, was undefeated in wrestling. Normally, he pinned his opponents in the first minute of the first round.

(**DUKE** *faces an opponent, trips him, leaps on his body, and pins him.*)

Florence, named after one of the greatest track stars of all time, Florence Griffith-Joyner, became a national champion at Tae Kwan Do. She was so good, her fellow students would only face her in a match if it was three against one.

(*Three tae kwan do students are knocked unconscious by* **FLORENCE.**)

Johnny, named after the toughest quarterback of all time, Johnny Unitas, pitched for his little league team and had a fastball that was clocked at eighty-miles an hour. Most of the batters he faced usually ran away.

(**JOHNNY** *is about to pitch, but the* **BATTER** *runs away.* **JOHNNY** *yells.*)

JOHNNY. Hey, where are you going?

(**JOHNNY** *runs after him, throws baseball he is holding; a loud "ow" is heard from* **BATTER** *off-stage.*)

NARRATOR. Then there was Billy Jean, named after the great female tennis player, Billy Jean King. She was a gymnast headed to be in the summer Olympics.

(**BILLY** *does a cartwheel and flips from one end of the stage to the other.*)

And then there was Rocky, who will, for all intents and purposes be referred to as Tenderfella the rest of our play. He was named after the fictional boxer, Rocky Balboa, but Rocky wasn't skilled at boxing, or running, or swimming, or anything that required athletic coordination. His strongest skill was showing empathy.

(**TENDERFELLA** *is talking on the phone.*)

TENDERFELLA. Look, Cindy, I know how you feel. It seems that no one understands you, but I do. You're a caring, loving, kind-hearted girl and you can't understand why people gossip about you. But you have to realize, those aren't your real friends. Real friends accept and love you for who you are. So you're feeling a little better? That's great! Call me anytime you need cheering up.

COACH. *(Enters)* What are you doing on the phone?

TENDERFELLA. There were some girls spreading rumors about Cindy; I needed to cheer her up.

COACH. Have you done your laps today?

TENDERFELLA. Ah, no.

COACH. Any sit ups?

TENDERFELLA. Not yet.

COACH. Push ups?

TENDERFELLA. Nope.

COACH. Any work on the weight machines?

TENDERFELLA. Sorry.

COACH. Sorry? You're sorry? How do you expect to stay in shape when all you do is talk on the phone? I've got news for you, picking up a telephone and putting it back down is not really working out. You'll never be able to play any sport if all you do is talk and talk and talk. You might as well get dinner ready. Chopping carrots and setting the table is probably the only exercise you're getting today!

TENDERFELLA. Yes, Father.

COACH. Call me Coach. You've got that? Coach! Tenderfella, I don't know what I'm going to do with you.

*(***TENDERFELLA*** brings out a table and sets it. The* **NARRATOR** *continues talking.)*

NARRATOR. I guess you could say that Tenderfella was a big disappointment to his family. He didn't enjoy playing sports. He didn't enjoy watching sports. He really didn't even like talking about sports. He did, however, like to write and recite poetry whenever he had the chance.

TENDERFELLA. Kindness and love embrace the soul and

spark a passion that achieves mystic fulfillment.

(**BILLY JEAN** *approaches* **TENDERFELLA** *with a look of pure disgust.*)

Light and dark, right and wrong, honesty and deception are part of an equation that...

(**BILLY JEAN** *cuts him off.*)

BILLY JEAN. Dad, Tenderfella is reciting poetry again.

(**COACH** *yells from off stage.*)

COACH. Tenderfella, cut it out and serve dinner, for heaven's sake!

NARRATOR. Coach insisted that dinner be served daily at 5:30. Everyone in the family was required to eat dinner together, no exceptions. Every day, Tenderfella set the table, prepared the dinner, and cleaned up afterwards. Since he wasn't involved in organized sports, Coach felt he was the only one who had the time to take care of the family's dinner. As you would expect, dinner conversation centered around sports.

(*The family is now sitting around the dinner table.*)

COACH. Anything interesting happen today kids?

ARNOLD. I got in trouble from the football coaching staff.

COACH. What did you do?

ARNOLD. The quarterback tried to take it up the middle and I slammed him good. Gave him a concussion; he missed the rest of the game.

COACH. And the problem is?

ARNOLD. Problem could be 'cuz he's our quarterback and can't play now.

COACH. If he can't take a hit, it's time for a new quarterback. How was your day, Duke?

DUKE. Today was a lot of fun. The wrestling team decided we'd practice with the chess team.

COACH. You mean the chess team wrestles?

DUKE. Not quite; we got a hold of the chess players and

squeezed four of 'em into a gym locker. It wasn't easy, either. Our P.E. teacher was pretty mad at us.

COACH. What's to be mad about? Boys will be boys. Florence, anything exciting in your life?

FLORENCE. We had a lot of fun at practice. Kuma John brought in a guest trainer today, Chuck Liddell.

COACH. Isn't he the world champion cage fighter?

FLORENCE. Yep. He squared off against me and told me to give him my best punch into his stomach. Instead, I gave him a roundhouse kick to his nose.

(Accidentally kicks a dish out of TENDERFELLA*'s hand.)*

I think I broke it.

COACH. That's my girl!

FLORENCE. The only problem is, he was supposed to fight next weekend for the championship. He has to postpone the match now. Kuma John was really mad; he made me do a hundred extra pull-ups.

COACH. I'll give him a call in the morning; punishing you is way out of line. Babe, didn't you have a game today?

BABE. We did.

COACH. And?

BABE. We won in the final ten seconds.

COACH. Did my girl score the winning goal?

BABE. Not this time. I only got the assist on the winning goal. I had a lousy game; only got two earlier goals and two assists. I think I was tired.

COACH. We all have our off days.

BILLY JEAN. Speaking of off days... I blew it on the parallel bars today.

COACH. What happened?

BILLY JEAN. I was in the middle of my routine and I sneezed.

JOHNNY. That's a coincidence. I sneezed, too. Right when I was throwing a fastball. I beaned the batter in the head. Their bench emptied and our bench emptied. It was quite a brawl. Man, it was fun!

COACH. You kids make your dad so proud! There isn't a coach alive as proud as I am of you!

(*TENDERFELLA walks over to everyone.*)

TENDERFELLA. How's dinner?

BILLY JEAN. The bread is stale!

JOHNNY. The soup is cold!

BABE. The vegetables are soggy!

ARNOLD. The meat is raw!

DUKE. The potatoes are hard!

FLORENCE. And the gravy has lumps in it!

COACH. Let's just skip the meal; what do you say we go get pizza tonight?

(*All the kids scream, "yes!"*)

TENDERFELLA. Can I clean up when we get home?

COACH. Not a chance. If there's any extra, we'll bring it back. You've got way too much cleaning to do. Let's go, kids.

(*All exit.*)

NARRATOR. (*Approaches* **TENDERFELLA** *as he's cleaning the dishes.*) And this was a typical evening for Tenderfella. A misfit in his own family. A boy without love. A four-teen carrot klutz. No chance of him ever having a normal relationship with his brothers and sisters.

TENDERFELLA. (*Sadly, to* **NARRATOR**.) Alright. They get the point.

NARRATOR. Sorry. (*To audience.*) I guess you get the point.

(*TENDERFELLA exits.*)

And yet, the cards of fate can sometimes change the fortune of any of us. The right cards were about to be dealt to Tenderfella. It happened at school. Third period P.E. to be exact. The physical education teacher, Mrs. Crenshaw, was teaching a hip hop unit. She tried to make her class relevant for her students. Next Saturday, the biggest event at Judkins High School was about to take place, the Valentine Sweetheart Dance. Everyone was scrambling for dates.

(*Three boys and a girl step out, holding cell phones.*)

MARK. (*On phone with* **GIRL 1.**) Hi Jennifer, this is Mark. I was wondering if you're available for the Sweetheart Dance.

JENNIFER. As a matter of fact, I am. Oh, hang on; my phone is beeping.

TOM. Hi, Jennifer, this is Tom. I know this is last minute, but the Sweetheart Dance is next Saturday. Are you by any chance available?

JENNIFER. You bet I am. Hang on for a minute. Uh, Mark, I forgot, I'm going to the dance with Tom.

MARK. Oh, that's alright; it sure would have been fun to go with you though.

JENNIFER. Hi, Tom, sorry to keep you waiting. Now, about that dance. Oh, hang on, my phone is beeping.

JOHN. Hi Jennifer, this is John. If you're still available, I'd love to take you to the Sweetheart Dance.

JENNIFER. Of course I'm available for you. Hang on a minute; I'm on the line with someone.
Hello, Tom, about the dance, I'm so sorry, John asked me weeks ago; it just slipped my mind.

TOM. I understand. I better hang up so I can see if anyone else is available.

JENNIFER. Buh bye. Hi there, John, I'm sure glad you called me, I was hoping I'd be going with you.

TOM. This is still Tom.

JENNIFER. Oh.

(*All four step back into the dance class.* **MRS. CRENSHAW** *is talking to the class.*)

CRENSHAW. Okay, ladies and gentlemen, if you want to impress your date at the Sweetheart Dance you're going to need a bit more rhythm. Let's try it again.

(*Turns on music, everyone begins to dance. After a few*

seconds, the music is turned off.)

That is not what I mean by rhythm. Tenderfella, can you please step out?

TENDERFELLA. Me?

CRENSHAW. Yes, you. I'd like you to demonstrate our dance for the class.

TENDERFELLA. You mean me?

CRENSHAW. Yes, Tenderfella, you. You might be uncoordinated at every sport invented by man, but you do seem to grasp the concept of hip hop dancing. So demonstrate, please.

(The music turns on and **TENDERFELLA** *begins to dance. As he is dancing, a new girl, who everyone recognizes as young actress,* **ROXANNE JANICO,** *enters.* **MRS. CRENSHAW** *turns off the music, but* **TENDERFELLA** *continues to dance.)*

NARRATOR. Just as Tenderfella was beginning to feel like he could actually do something right, everyone at Judkins High was stunned to learn that the famous child actress, Roxanne Janico, had just enrolled in their school. All eyes were riveted on Roxanne.

*(***NARRATOR** *yells in* **TENDERFELLA***'s ear.)*

I said all eyes.

*(***TENDERFELLA** *stops and also looks at* **ROXANNE***.)*

Roxanne, who has made music videos, films, and now was a star on the hit soap opera, "Our Days Are Numbered," handed Mrs. Crenshaw her new enrollment form.

CRENSHAW. And what brings us the pleasure of having you at our school, Miss Janico?

NARRATOR. Here's how the pleasure came about. Roxanne was in Hollywood, filming another episode of "Our Days Are Numbered." They were on a deadline to finish filming and she had been working for fifteen straight hours. Let's just say Roxanne and the director were having creative differences.

(The gym class exits; a film crew enters. The **DIREC-TOR**'s *arm is around* **ROXANNE**.*)*

DIRECTOR. Listen Roxanne, I don't believe you have explored Sasha's character enough. Your lines are coming out flat. Let's review the scene. Sasha has just discovered that her father, Melvin, was married to her Aunt Velma. Velma, as you know, has been committed to a hospital for the criminally insane for stealing her cousin's baby, Theo. Remember, Theo is the only white gang member of the Crips. The Crips have just kidnapped your real mother and are demanding ransom money. You are enraged, and you have sought out Theo, begging for the safe return of your mother. So you are upset, angry, confused, and hurt while you confront Theo. Let's try it again. And... action!

*(**ROXANNE** confronts **THEO**.)*

ROXANNE. *(To* **THEO***)* Theo, I can't believe you are involved with this.

DIRECTOR. Cut! I can't believe you're involved with this. Take two. And...action.

ROXANNE. Theo, I can't believe you're involved with this.

DIRECTOR. Cut. Emphasize you're, I can't believe YOU'RE involved with this. Take three. And action.

ROXANNE. Theo, I can't believe YOU'RE involved with this.

DIRECTOR. Cut. Too much emphasis on YOU'RE.

ROXANNE. For cryin' out loud. Can we just run the scene without you interrupting?

DIRECTOR. Oh, by all means, Roxanne, let's just run the scene. In fact, you probably don't need me at all. I've only been directing feature films and television shows for the last twenty years; what could I possibly know compared to a fourteen year old know-it-all?

ROXANNE. Just run the scene, okay?

DIRECTOR. You heard the primadonna, everyone. Take

four. Action.

ROXANNE. Theo, I can't believe you're involved with this. We're family. We have a blood relationship. How could you forsake that?

THEO. Yo, sister, it's out with the old blood and in with the new.

ROXANNE. How would you feel if this was your mother?

THEO. Whoa. We're not talking my mama, we're talking yo mama.

ROXANNE. But it could be YO mama.

THEO. You're just not jiving with the facts, girl, it's YO mama and that's all there is to it.

ROXANNE. *(Pulling out a gun.)* Listen, Theo, I want my mama back or you're never going to see your mama again.

THEO. Girl, relax. You shoot me and you'll never see yo mama again.

NARRATOR. In the middle of the scene, Roxanne stopped, looked at the director and chucked her entire acting career.

ROXANNE. *(To the* **DIRECTOR.** *)* These lines are ridiculous! This entire television show is ridiculous. I quit! I want to get out of Hollywood and move where people are real. I want to be a normal teenage kid. *(She exits.)*

NARRATOR. And off Roxanne went. Of course, we know living a normal teenage life is much more difficult after becoming a movie and television star. Roxanne has fans everywhere.

(A **FAN** *runs out on stage.)*

FAN. I heard Roxanne Janico is in the building. Can someone tell me where? I've watched all her movies, like five times each. She's beautiful, talented and famous. She's everything I've always wanted to be. When she was in that movie where her boyfriend told her he's leaving her for good, I'll never forget her answer. "Fine!" That's what she said. "Fine!" No one delivers lines with as much conviction as Roxanne. She is my hero, and I heard she's in the building! I have to find her, I just have to. *(Runs off stage.)*

NARRATOR. While Roxanne wanted to move on with her life, Roxanne's mother was a different story. Hollywood stars are treated like royalty, and Mrs. Janico was kinda used to it.

MRS. JANICO. *(Following* **ROXANNE** *in.)* But Honey, be reasonable. Let's just take a nice vacation to Hawaii or Costa Rica. Better yet, we'll rent a villa in the South of France. You'll feel better then.

ROXANNE. You don't get it, Mother. I don't want to act anymore. It's fake, and I don't like it.

MRS. JANICO. Come on, Roxanne, a lot of things are fake.

ROXANNE. Like what?

MRS. JANICO. Like, like make-up. Girls everywhere apply tons of make-up to change their looks. And hair, oh my! Pink, green, red, rainbow; who has natural hair these days?

ROXANNE. I'm not talking about hair and make-up. I'm talking about a different life.

MRS. JANICO. And where is this new life going to be?

ROXANNE. North. I want to go as far north as possible. And I want to go to a public school with normal kids.

MRS. JANICO. Darling, a public school? They take anybody there. If you want to move north of Hollywood why don't we move to Encino; you can enroll at Buckley School and meet kids with more to offer.

ROXANNE. I don't want to go to another private school, and I don't want to move to Encino. I want to go to a small town where no one knows my name. And I want to go as far north as it takes.

*(***ROXANNE*** exits.)*

MRS. JANICO. *(Calling out to her.)* Fine, if you want to forsake your career, it's your life. We better call your agent; he's going to love this.

NARRATOR. Roxanne quitting Hollywood affected a lot of

people. While everyone had to know what was going on, not everyone had to get the same story. When Mrs. Janico called Roxanne's agent, at first he was incredulous, then nervous, and finally, angry. No agent likes to give up ten percent, especially when we're talking millions of dollars.

AGENT. You're telling me Roxanne is going to chuck her career for the sake of living her life like the characters in the defunct TV show, Northern Exposure? Hey, wait a minute, I hear they're gonna do a remake of Northern Exposure. Why don't you ask Roxanne if she wants to audition for a part? That way her acting life will be like how she wants her real life to be.

MRS. JANICO. I'm afraid there's no choice. When Roxanne makes up her mind, nothing can change it. (MRS. JANICO exits.)

AGENT. I'll give the studio a call. I don't think they're gonna like it.

(Calls studio. MAX, a studio executive, picks up the phone.)

Max, Baby, how are you doing?

MAX. Every time you say, "Max, Baby," something is wrong. Let's cut to the chase. What do you want?

AGENT. Oh, believe me, it's not what I want; it's what Roxanne Janico wants.

MAX. What about her?

AGENT. She's leaving the show.

MAX. What do you mean she's leaving the show? She's got a contract. I'm not paying her another dime. If she leaves the show, she'll never work in Hollywood again.

AGENT. I'm afraid that's how she'd prefer it.

MAX. Prefer it? What kid in her right mind would not want to be working in Hollywood?

AGENT. She's having a nervous breakdown and we've got to let her mend.

MAX. Fourteen-year-old girls have no right to have nervous

breakdowns. They haven't been around enough. After forty, fifty years, nervous breakdowns are fine; but not when you're the hottest star on television.

AGENT. Give it time, she'll be back.

MAX. Well, I'm going to have to call the executive producer; she won't like this one bit.

(**AGENT** *leaves;* **MAX** *dials producer.*)

Now don't get mad at me; I let you know as soon as I heard. Roxanne had to quit the show and leave town.

PRODUCER. She's left town and quit the show. What are you telling me? I can't replace her in the middle of the season.

MAX. Sorry, no choice; you're going to have to replace her.

PRODUCER. You don't think the audience will notice when the leading star becomes a complete different person one week later?

MAX. Hey, the audience didn't know when they switched Lassie.

PRODUCER. Lassie's a dog, Max; Roxanne is a teenage phenomenon. Believe me, the audience will notice.

MAX. Look, here's the story: Roxanne had to leave to receive some experimental treatment for a disorder that is affecting her ability to function.

PRODUCER. What's the disorder?

MAX. Not certain, but we're positive she'll recover. She just needs some time. I told you she'd make your show the number one hit, and she has. Just give her some time to recover.

PRODUCER. Oh, man, I don't know what I'm going to say to the director.

MAX. I'm sure you'll think of something.

(**MAX** *leaves; the* **PRODUCER** *calls the* **DIRECTOR.**)

DIRECTOR. Hello.

PRODUCER. I'm going to say this as fast as possible so it will be less painful; Roxanne will not be able to finish the season.

DIRECTOR. What?!

PRODUCER. We did everything we could. But she is on life support as we speak.

DIRECTOR. Don't con me, she walked out on me.

PRODUCER. And promptly had a brain aneurysm. That's why she was acting so strange. Listen, she'll be back when she can. She moved north for a while.

DIRECTOR. She had to go north, poor girl.

(Both exit.)

NARRATOR. *(The P.E. class returns.)* And that's how Roxanne ended up in Pismo Beach. Mrs. Janico discovered it was a friendly small town with great public schools, and yet close enough to get back to Los Angeles should Roxanne have a change of heart. Of course, Roxanne really was naive to think she could go anywhere without making a commotion.

ROXANNE. All right, I get it; all of you are staring at me because you think you know who I am. I'm not her, okay? I'm someone who wants to go to school and be Roxanne Janico, Nobody. Can I please be that girl?

(Everyone stops staring and **MRS. CRENSHAW** *continues talking.)*

CRENSHAW. Okay, that will be it; I'll see everyone tomorrow.

(Everyone starts to leave; **CRENSHAW** *signals for* **ROXANNE** *to come over.)*

Miss Janico, I know you don't want everyone to make a big deal over who you are, but it is a big deal. Rather than fighting with the person you have become, see if you can accept that person.

ROXANNE. I'll try, Mrs. Crenshaw.

*(***CRENSHAW** *exits.* **ROXANNE** *takes out her schedule and looks at it as the narrator addresses the audience.)*

NARRATOR. So Roxanne tried to be a normal kid, but the

reaction her fellow Judkins students had towards her was unnerving.

(Two boys walk up, awkwardly stare at her, then say, "hi." Several students walk by her and point, giggle, and stare. Three girls walk past **ROXANNE** *and one of them quips, "She's not that good looking in person."* **ROXANNE** *starts to exit stage left and encounters four* **CHEERLEADERS**.*)*

CHEERLEADER 1. Hi, Roxanne, how are you?

ROXANNE. Just fine.

CHEERLEADER 2. All of us wanted to say we're glad you came to our school.

CHEERLEADER 3. Hopefully, you'll like it here. Maybe you want to even be a cheerleader.

(The **CHEERLEADERS**, *trying to impress Roxanne, perform a quick routine.)*

CHEERLEADER 4. Yeah, maybe we could talk to our advisor and she, you know, will still let you join; or at least try out, since you weren't here for the real tryouts.

ROXANNE. No thanks, I really don't want any extra commitments.

CHEERLEADER 1. Oh, but being a cheerleader gives you top status around this place. Cheerers are leaders, you know.

ROXANNE. Just the same, I'll pass for now.

CHEERLEADER 4. Let us know if you change your mind; see ya.

*(*CHEERLEADERS *exit.)*

ROXANNE. I just want to be a normal kid.

(Walks to a bench and sits down. She moves a lunch bag, which was left on the bench. **TENDERFELLA** comes over and picks up bag.)*

I'm sorry, I didn't realize that was your lunch.

TENDERFELLA. It's okay. I'll go and eat somewhere else.

ROXANNE. No, please, sit here. I was just about to go.

TENDERFELLA. It's fine if you go, I'm kind of used to being alone.

ROXANNE. You know what's weird? I always have people around me. And I can't go anywhere without people gathering around me; and still, I feel alone, too.

TENDERFELLA. I always thought famous people had millions of friends.

ROXANNE. Fans maybe, but friends are hard to come by. So how come you don't act different around me?

TENDERFELLA. Excuse me?

ROXANNE. You don't act as if talking to me is a big deal.

TENDERFELLA. Actually, talking to anyone is a big deal to me. You just seem, well, normal.

ROXANNE. That's the nicest thing anyone has ever said to me! *(She hugs him.)*

(WILLARD, and a few of his friends, walk in as TENDERFELLA is getting hugged.)

WILLARD. Hey, Roxanne, you don't want to hug him; you might catch what he has.

ROXANNE. What are you talking about?

WILLARD. Look at him, he's a teenage weasel. If you're giving out hugs, well, I'm your man.

ROXANNE. Really? Come here, Handsome.

WILLARD. My pleasure.

(WILLARD comes in for a hug and ROXANNE knees him in the stomach. He bends over in pain.)

What'd you do that for?

ROXANNE. I always like to give people what they deserve.

WILLARD. You're crazy, I'm gonna burn all of your DVDs when I get home!

(He exits with his friends.)

TENDERFELLA. That was pretty awesome.

ROXANNE. I can't stand bullies. Here's a little secret; I wasn't the most popular kid in school, either. Once I started to act, though, people treated me differently. I'd give anything to be a kid nobody recognized now. I better get going; it was nice talking to you. See ya around.

(**ROXANNE** *and* **TENDERFELLA** *exit. The* **NARRATOR** *resumes speaking.*)

NARRATOR. Unfortunately for Roxanne, her life of anonymity was over. Wherever she moved, she'd cause a ruckus. Moving to Pismo Beach just before the Sweetheart Dance was not exactly the best timing; the burning question was would Roxanne Janico attend the dance, and if she did, with whom?

(*Lights dim and a talk radio show is heard.*)

RADIO HOST. Welcome, once again, to Missy's Report. Today we have an interesting topic; will anybody in Pismo Beach be lucky enough to take Roxanne Janico to the Sweetheart Dance? The Sweetheart Dance, as you know, is a huge event. It's been a tradition at Judkins High for over forty years. Every kid in the community is scrambling for a date. That, in itself, is not news. Asking Roxanne Janico to it is. Roxanne has starred in several motion pictures, "Walking on Eggshells," "Teen Dreams," and the remake of "Mr. Ed." Studio officials were taken by surprise when she relocated to Pismo Beach and left the hit television show, "Our Days Are Numbered." So what does our studio audience think about this?

AUDIENCE MEMBER 1. I live in Pismo Beach and I just wanted Roxanne to know that I think she'll find our area inviting, hospitable, and a welcome release from the pressures of Los Angeles. And Roxanne, if you're listening, my son's name is Tommy Anderson, and he'd be proud as punch to escort you to the dance. He's a great boy, Roxanne, don't miss the opportunity.

HOST. Thanks for your input, let's try another caller.

AUDIENCE MEMBER 2. Hi, Dave, this is Freddy Wilcox; I'm a student at Judkins High. I just wanted to tell you that

I love your show; listen to it every day. I have a message for Roxanne. I love you, Baby; you're the best. The dance is coming up. Will you be my sweetheart, Roxanne, huh, will you?

HOST. Freddy, it's going to be hard for Roxanne to find a better offer than that. Ladies and Gentleman, we're going to take a short break; it seems we have so many callers, all of our phone lines are tied up.

(Lights fade back to **TENDERFELLA** *serving dinner to his family.* **COACH** *is reading a newspaper as he begins speaking to his kids.)*

COACH. Guess what the leading story in the Tribune is today kids?

DUKE. Peace in Iraq.

COACH. Not yet.

BABE. Solutions to Global Warming.

COACH. They're still looking.

ARNOLD. A new scandal in Washington.

COACH. Not today.

FLORENCE. The economy is on the rebound.

COACH. Not my investments.

JOHNNY. Los Angeles is getting a football team.

COACH. Los Angeles is a Laker town!

BILLY JEAN. A new exciting presidential candidate.

COACH. After our current president, anyone would be exciting. Boys and girls, how can you be so out of touch, especially when it affects your own lives? The lead story couldn't be more important, "WILL ROXANNE JANICO ATTEND THE SWEETHEART DANCE?" Well, will she?

ARNOLD. Gee, Coach, I don't know. Most of the guys have dates already.

COACH. Who's your date?

ARNOLD. Brenda Cooper, the hottest cheerleader on the squad.

COACH. And what about you, Duke?

DUKE. I'm going with Amanda Jenson, you know, the girl who was runner up in the Miss Teenage Beauty Pageant.

COACH. And you, Johnny?

JOHNNY. I'm going with my girlfriend, Donna, the one I've been dating for the last two years.

COACH. Get on the phone and cancel your dates.

BOYS. Coach!

COACH. No backtalk. Do you know what a date with Roxanne Janico would mean to our family? Interviews with the newspapers, public adulation. Who knows, she might move back to Hollywood and take one of you with her. When opportunity knocks, ya gotta open the door. Listen, Babe, you work with Duke, Florence with Arnold, and Billy Jean with Johnny. Each of you devise a plan to entice and win Roxanne's heart. Among the three of you, someone has to succeed.

(COACH *looks at his fork and yells at* TENDERFELLA.)

Tenderfella, look at this fork.

(TENDERFELLA *walks over.*)

TENDERFELLA. Is there a problem?

COACH. Is there a problem? Is there a problem? Yes, there's a problem! There's dried egg yolk stuck in between the fork blades. Since you can't even play one sport, I'd hope at least you'd be able to wash dishes. You're grounded this weekend; I want you to polish all the silver!

TENDERFELLA. But on Saturday I was hoping to go to the Sweetheart Dance.

COACH. Well, you can forget it; you'll be home learning responsibility. *(Laughs.)* Besides, who'd be your sweetheart? Let's go out and get some pizza, kids. Tenderfella's got me sick to my stomach. *(To* TENDERFELLA*)* Don't expect any pizza; if you get hungry, eat the yoke off the fork. *(As they exit)* On the way, boys, call off your dates; it's time to focus only on Roxanne.

BOYS. *(As they exit the* **BOYS** *lament)* They're gonna be really mad!

(Three girls, **BRENDA, AMANDA** *and* **DONNA** *are on their cell phones. They speak one after the other.)*

BRENDA. What

AMANDA. do

DONNA. you

BRENDA. mean

AMANDA. you're

DONNA. going

BRENDA. to

AMANDA. cancel

DONNA. our

BRENDA. date

AMANDA. to

DONNA. the

BRENDA. Sweetheart

AMANDA. Dance?!

DONNA. Are

BRENDA. you

AMANDA. crazy?!

DONNA. We've

BRENDA. had

AMANDA. this

DONNA. planned

BRENDA. for

AMANDA. a

DONNA. year!

BRENDA. I

AMANDA. don't

DONNA. ever

BRENDA. want

AMANDA. to

DONNA. talk

BRENDA. to

AMANDA. you

DONNA. again!

ALL THREE. Creep!

(The **NARRATOR** *comes out with students at Judkins High.)*

NARRATOR. On a side note, there is a terrible misconception that public schools are simply not doing their job. The measurement, which is called "No Child Left Behind," was designed by President Bush and proposes that every child in the nation be proficient in language, math, science and history by the year 2014. Around the same time, our country will no longer have crime, poverty, greenhouse emissions, global warming or defiant teenagers. There is no doubt that what takes place in the classroom is critical to the success of every child in America; however, what takes place at lunch is equally important.

*(*NARRATOR *moves to the various groups eating their lunches or just talking.)*

Over here we have a couple of girls practicing the art of make-up design. Every color they choose, every line they apply has been planned, analyzed, and practiced. And the outcome is obvious to anyone around.

(A **BOY** *walks up to the girls who have just applied their makeup.)*

BOY. Jennifer, what's wrong with your face?

NARRATOR. *(Walking up to another couple of students.)* And here you see a couple of boys in the Chess Club practicing their craft. This particular game they're involved in has been battled for the last two weeks. Oh, and here comes the school bully, Willard, to see what's transpiring.

WILLARD. *(As he knocks the chessboard over.)* Oops! *(Walks off laughing.)*

NARRATOR. This just isn't a lesson about bullying. It's about the future. You see, Albert, the object of Willard's torment, will go on to establish an important computer company. And Willard, will find his financial survival in Albert's hand.

(ALBERT starts talking on the phone. WILLARD is shining his shoes.)

ALBERT. What do you mean Google out performed us last month? Google is a dinosaur. You get all of our computer programmers in a room and you communicate this message for me. If our performance doesn't improve next week, there are a lot of unemployed programmers who would love to show me what they can do. I want production, not excuses.

(Looks at WILLARD for the first time.)

Were you listening in on that conversation, Willard?

WILLARD. Yes, Sir! I mean, no. Sir! I mean, sort of, Sir.

ALBERT. Well, maybe you heard the part about production. That means doing your job correctly. Look at my left shoe, Willard. You missed a scuff mark. I'll be going to a meeting with Bill Gates with a scuff mark on my left shoe. I don't know why I keep you around here.

(ALBERT tosses his shoe shining equipment in the air; WILLARD scurries to pick it up.)

WILLARD. I'll do better next time. Sir. I promise. *(He exits)*

NARRATOR. *(Walks to a couple of GIRLS on cell phones.)* What's taking place in this corner of the cafeteria is two girls practicing the art of interpersonal communication via their cell phones. It's called text messaging.

GIRL 1. Hey, what's up?

GIRL 2. Nothing, looking for something to do.

GIRL 1. Well, now U R doing something…talking to me. lol.

GIRL 2. So isn't the new kid at school, Roxanne Janico, annoying? It's like every guy thinks she's all that.

GIRL 1. You sound jealous.

GIRL 2. I do not.

GIRL 1. Actually, you do.

GIRL 2. Speaking of jealous, did you hear that Arnold, Johnny, and Duke canceled their dates with Amanda, Brenda, and Donna?

GIRL 1. No way!

GIRL 2. Yes way. They're in some kind of contest to get a date with Roxanne for the Sweetheart Dance.

GIRL 1. I'd be so mad. lol.

GIRL 2. Me, too. lol.

NARRATOR. So you get the point. A lot of stuff happens at lunch.

(**ROXANNE** *enters and joins a group of students.*)

Oh, Roxanne just entered; we better get back to our story. You can see for yourself that Babe and Duke are ready for their move; we might as well watch.

BABE. Now let's review our plan. Go up to Roxanne and don't act nervous. All you have to do is talk about roses. I guarantee that's all you are going to need to do. Every girl loves roses.

DUKE. But I don't know anything about roses except they got thorns, smell good, and come in different colors.

BABE. Look over the information I gave you.

DUKE. There's way too much to read.

BABE. Just learn the stuff that will help.

DUKE. What good is it going to do to tell her, "Roses are supplied bare-root for planting from November to March and are robust, lightweight and easy to handle"?

BABE. That's not what I want you to look at. First, you read her this poem. "The rose is gowned in petaled grace and lovely beyond telling; She always lifts a friendly grace, regardless of her dwelling." And then you hand her this pink rose, which is called a Rainbow Knockout, and this white rose, called a Moondance, and you point out their exceptional delightful fragrance, and how there is no other flower in the world as romantic. These are not ordinary roses. They won an international competition and are quite valuable; don't waste them. I expect you to get a date. Now go get her!

DUKE. *(Awkwardly taps* **ROXANNE** *on the shoulder)* Excuse me, I just wanted to show you a moon dance and then have a rainbow knock you out.

ROXANNE. *(Confused)* Excuse me?

DUKE. That's not what I meant. What I meant is, this rose is pedaling without telling, because its friendly face lives without a dwelling.

ROXANNE. What's that supposed to mean?

DUKE. I just wanted to give you these roses and ask you to the dance.

(He hands her the roses, but then appears to be grimacing in pain.)

ROXANNE. You put your hand around the thorns, huh?

*(**DUKE** nods his head up and down.)*

Under normal circumstances, I'd love the roses, but I'm afraid if I took them, you'd start bleeding. Maybe you should go to a doctor. I'm not sure I want to go to the dance, okay?

*(Again, nods in agreement and then walks to **BABE** and whispers in her ear.)*

BABE. You did what? That was a waste of two award winning roses.

(They both exit.

FLORENCE *and* **ARNOLD** *walk in arguing.)*

ARNOLD. I can't do it. I can't walk up to a movie star and ask her to the Sweetheart Dance. I'm not good at this kind of stuff.

FLORENCE. You don't have a choice. Coach told us to give it our best shot and that's what we're going to do.

ARNOLD. I am telling you, I'll be tongue-tied and sound

like a babbling idiot.

FLORENCE. Like I don't know that. Here, put these head phones on and I'll feed you the lines. It'll be just like Cyrano de Bergerac.

ARNOLD. I can't speak French.

FLORENCE. Just go up and talk to her and leave the rest to me. Make sure you say what I say, exactly.

(ARNOLD *goes up to* ROXANNE.)

Now tap her on the shoulder.

ARNOLD. Now, I'll tap you on the shoulder.

ROXANNE. *(Turning around.)* What did you say?

FLORENCE. Don't tell her you're going to tap her on the shoulder; you should have just tapped her on the shoulder.

ARNOLD. I didn't mean to tell you I was going to tap you on the shoulder, I just meant to tap you on the shoulder.

FLORENCE. Stop talking about tapping her shoulder.

ARNOLD. I'm going to stop talking about your shoulder now.

FLORENCE. Don't repeat anything I say for the next few seconds.

(ARNOLD *is now just staring at* ROXANNE.)

ROXANNE. Are you okay?

(ARNOLD *continues to stare.*)

FLORENCE. Tell her you're fine and you were so captivated by her beauty you didn't know what to say.

(ARNOLD *continues to stare.*)

ROXANNE. You're making me very uncomfortable.

FLORENCE. This is turning into a disaster. Let's try it again before it's too late. I'll speak slowly; repeat what I say. Listen, Roxanne?

ARNOLD. Listen, Roxanne.

FLORENCE. You know the Sweetheart Dance is coming up.

ARNOLD. You know the Sweetheart Dance is coming up.

FLORENCE. It's a tradition for couples with the right chemistry to...

ARNOLD. It's a tradition for couples with the right chemistry to...

FLORENCE. Arnold! Oh no! The batteries just died! Arnold, can you hear me? Can you hear me?

ROXANNE. What was that you were saying about chemistry?

ARNOLD. Florence! Florence! Chemistry! Help, please! Yes, chemistry! I was talking about chemistry, correct?

ROXANNE. You were talking about some kind of tradition for couples with chemistry.

ARNOLD. Okay, here's the thing about chemistry.

(Desperately speaks into the headset one last time.)

Florence, help.

*(**ARNOLD** sees **FLORENCE** mouth the words, "The batteries are dead. You're on your own." **ARNOLD** mouths back, "What?" He turns and faces **ROXANNE**.)*

You know that a lot of students can't even pass chemistry, let alone use it in their lives. I, however, have found a way to use it.

ROXANNE. And...

ARNOLD. And, and, I can use it at the Sweetheart Dance. I can study chemistry, with you.

ROXANNE. Why would I want to study chemistry at the Sweetheart Dance?

ARNOLD. Not exactly study it, more like live it. What I mean to say is the chemistry we share can be brought together and ignited at the dance.

ROXANNE. First, I barely know you, let alone feel any chemistry. Second, I'm not interested in the Sweetheart Dance. And third, next time you talk to me, make sure your headset works.

*(**ROXANNE** walks back to a group of students.)*

ARNOLD. *(Backing up slowly.)* I'll do that, I'll get batteries that work. It was very nice talking with you.

(Looks at **FLORENCE** *and utters under his breath.)*

Thanks a lot.

(They walk off together arguing as **BILLY JEAN** *and* **JOHNNY** *enter.)*

BILLY JEAN. *(Speaking to* **JOHNNY.**) We'll do this together. We'll strike up a normal conversation, talk about the weather, whatever, and then we'll get around to your muscles. Girls love guys with big muscles. Then just talk about how you work out and stay in shape and before you know it, you have a new date to the Sweetheart Dance. Now put up your arms.

JOHNNY. What for?

BILLY JEAN. *(Squirts water under his arm pits and on his chest.)* So it looks like you're coming back from a strenuous work-out.

JOHNNY. Are you sure about this?

BILLY JEAN. Trust me.

(Walks up to **ROXANNE** *and pulls her from her friends.)*

Roxanne, my brother and I really haven't had the opportunity to say hi. Hi.

JOHNNY. Hey.

ROXANNE. And you are, again?

BILLY JEAN. Oh, yeah, I'm Billy Jean, and this is Johnny.

JOHNNY. Hey.

BILLY JEAN. You were talking to my other brothers and sisters just a few minutes ago. You know, Babe, Arnold, Duke, and Florence.

ROXANNE. I remember. Don't you have another brother, too?

BILLY JEAN. You mean, Tenderfella. I wouldn't call him a brother; he's more like a mutant.

ROXANNE. I think he's one of the nicest boys at this school!

BILLY JEAN. If you want to see something really nice, check out Johnny's biceps.

(**BILLY JEAN** *feels his biceps.*)

No steroids for him, you're looking at the real McCoy.

ROXANNE. I've never been a fan of big muscles. They seem artificial.

BILLY JEAN. How can you say that? Johnny, pose for Roxanne.

(**JOHNNY** *strikes up several "muscle man" poses.*)

ROXANNE. I've got to tell you, that does nothing for me, except maybe make me sick to my stomach. And that sweat under his arms and on his chest, gross!

BILLY JEAN. So going out with my brother to the Sweetheart Dance would be out of the question?

ROXANNE. Definitely. See ya.

(*She turns away to a group of students.*)

BILLY JEAN. See ya.

JOHNNY. Hey.

(**BILLY JEAN** *takes his arm and escorts him out.*

TENDERFELLA *walks in, looking at a book, and approaches* **ROXANNE.**)

TENDERFELLA. Hi, Roxanne.

ROXANNE. (*Turning towards* **TENDERFELLA**) Hello.

TENDERFELLA. I just want to...

ROXANNE. Let me guess, you're going to give me some kind ridiculous line that will win me over so I'll go to the dance with you. What's with your family? They seem to be having some kind of contest and I'm the prize.

TENDERFELLA. I'm sorry about that. I didn't come here about the dance. I'm not allowed to go. I just wrote a book of poetry. I thought you'd want to read some of my poems. Never mind, though.

(*He starts to walk off.*)

ROXANNE. Tenderfella, I didn't mean to be rude. I'd love to read your poems.

TENDERFELLA. Are you sure?

ROXANNE. Of course I am! *(She takes book.)*

TENDERFELLA. You can give it back to me whenever you want. I've got to go; see you soon.

ROXANNE. Bye.

(She glances at book and reads a poem as she exits.)

"Everyone shines for a moment. Fame and failure, truth and deception fill our void on the stage of life."

*(The **NARRATOR** returns to center stage and continues his tale.)*

NARRATOR. In no time at all, the Sweetheart Dance arrived. Everyone who was anyone was anxiously getting ready.

(Several actors and actresses cross the stage in frantic preparation.)

Roxanne decided to stay home and read Tenderfella's poems, and Tenderfella, well, he had some silverware to polish. Coach was not happy with any of his children.

*(While **TENDERFELLA** is polishing the silverware, the other children are doing jumping jacks as **COACH** yells at them.)*

COACH. So none of my sons gets a date with Roxanne Janico; nice work! I hope you enjoy the dance tonight.

(The kids stop doing jumping jacks.)

BILLY JEAN. It stinks that Johnny, my own brother, has to be my date now!

BABE. Well, I have to go with Arnold!

FLORENCE. And I have to go with Duke!

COACH. No complaining, it could have been worse; you could be going with Tenderfella. Now get in the minivan and let's get a move on it.

FLORENCE. *(Sarcastic.)* This is going to be a fun dance!

*(They all exit. **COACH** looks at **TENDERFELLA** and gives one last order.)*

COACH. Make sure that silverware is spotless when we get back!

(He exits and **TENDERFELLA** *is left polishing the silverware. The* **AGENT**, *with wings on his back, enters.)*

AGENT. Are you the kid they call Tenderfella?

TENDERFELLA. That's me.

AGENT. We need to get going; we've got an engagement.

TENDERFELLA. As you can see, I have a job tonight; if this doesn't get done, I'm in big trouble. Who are you, anyway?

AGENT. Just call me your fairy godfather; I even got the wings to prove it.

TENDERFELLA. Why do you have wings?

AGENT. I was at a costume party with my kid, and forgot to remove 'em. Let's go, we've got a Sweetheart Dance to attend.

TENDERFELLA. What about the silverware?

AGENT. Leave it to me, now go change.

*(**TENDERFELLA** exits. The* **AGENT** *dials a number on his phone and barks instructions to an assistant.)*

Hey, Gloria. I'm fine, no time for chit chat. I need you to get on the phone with Macy's and have some new silverware delivered to Pismo Beach. I don't care if they're closed; figure it out, that's what I pay you for! I need silverware in two hours, comprende? Good.

*(**TENDERFELLA** appears, dressed for the dance.)*

Get in my Beamer. First we have to go by and pick up Roxanne.

TENDERFELLA. Roxanne?

AGENT. I'll explain on the way.

(They exit and the set changes to the Sweetheart dance. Couples are dancing. An **ANNOUNCER** *steps out and begins to speak.)*

ANNOUNCER. Ladies and gentlemen, our next dance will determine the king and queen of this year's Sweetheart Dance. If you are tapped, stand to the side and wait to see who will be the "Sweetheart Couple of the

Year." Music, please.

(The music comes on and the dance begins. TENDER-
FELLA and ROXANNE arrive and join in. Eventually,
everyone is tapped out, except TENDERFELLA and ROX-
ANNE. The music stops and the announcer calls out the
winners.)

Congratulations to Tenderfella and Roxanne!

(At first, everyone is stunned, and then an enthusiastic
applause begins. COACH grabs TENDERFELLA by the
arm and loudly whispers...)

COACH. What are you doing here? You had work to do!

(The AGENT grabs the mic and begins speaking.)

AGENT. I, also, would like to make a bit of an announce-
ment. Steven Spielberg wanted to get back to
sentimental movie-making and sent me over a script.
It's about an actress who wants to move away from Hollywood because she is unhappy. She moves away to a
small town, finds her soulmate, and returns to Hollywood, realizing it's not where you are, it's who you're
with. Spielberg wants Roxanne Janico for this part.
She agreed under one condition, Tenderfella plays the
leading man. Spielberg agreed, and you are now looking at the couple that's going to make the biggest hit
since "High School Musical!"

(Again, everyone applauds enthusiastically. The AGENT
walks to COACH.)

I'll need your signature as his guardian, if you don't
have any objections.

COACH. Objections, no, no, it sounds... amazing.

AGENT. Tenderfella's in for the time of his life.

COACH. *(Proudly.)* My son's name is Rocky, Rocky Ackerson.

AGENT. Let's go over the details of his contract, if you don't
mind.

(Puts his arm around COACH and walks off. Everyone
leaves the dance and the NARRATOR takes center stage.)

NARRATOR. And that's our story about love, happiness, and success. Even in a small town like Pismo Beach, dreams can come true.

(The NARRATOR exits and COACH enters, talking on the phone. In the background, COACH's children are setting the table and preparing dinner.)

COACH. Rocky, how are you? How's the filming going? That's great. Hey, have you had an opportunity to tell Mr. Spielberg about my idea? You know, the one where a coach of a Pop Warner football team takes over the Green Bay Packers and they win the Super Bowl? Well, if you get the chance, let him know. It'd be a great movie!

(COACH turns to his children, who are preparing dinner, and starts yelling.)

That dinner looks like slop! And look at the plates and silverware, did any of you think about washing them? Can't the six of you figure out how to make a decent meal? Rocky could do better alone and blind folded! Hey Rocky, let me know when you'll be in town; I'd sure like to take you out for some pizza!

(Lights fade.)

COSTUME PLOT

NARRATOR:
          Formal outfit

ANNETTE:
          Business outfit

JOSH:
               Turtleneck shirt
               Slacks

CHEERLEADERS:
               Cheerleading uniform

STUDENTS AT JUDKINS HIGH:
               Casual clothing
               P.E. uniforms

FOOTBALL TEAM:
               Jerseys and helmets

COACH:
               Sweatpants
               Tennis shoes
               Green Bay Packer shirt

COACH'S WIFE:
               A plain and matronly outfit

TENDERFELLA:
               Dress shirt
               Dress slacks
               Suspenders

ROXANNE:
               Colorful blouse
               Tight pants

DIRECTOR, AGENT, MAX AND PRODUCER
               Flamboyant and trendy outfits

BILLY JEAN, ARNOLD, DUKE, FLORENCE, BABE AND JOHNNY:
               Appropriate athletic clothes when introduced by Narrator
(Johnny, baseball   uniform, Babe, soccer, etc…)

THEO
               Oversized pants, headband and tee shirt.

MRS. JANICO
               Stylish dress

PROPS

Briefcase
Camera
Deck of cards
Ant farm
Bug Spray
Baby stroller
Bowling bowl
Whistle
Football
Baseball, bat and glove
Soccer ball
Composition book for Tenderfella's poetry
Bench
Portable picnic table for scenes at dinner table
Plates and food and silverware
Bench
4 cell phones
Chessboard
Shoe shine kit
Various make-up
1 white rose and 1 pink rose
Two head sets
Spray bottle
Angel wings

SET PLOT

Tenderfella can be performed on an empty set with minimal props. The only necessary furniture is a portable dinner table. For added effect and if a backdrop is available to paint on, *Tenderfella* can be written into a hillside with two spot lights directed up (like the Hollywood sign). When Roxanne and Tenderfella fall in love, fiber optic lighting in the shape of a heart can be turned on as the lights dim. Christmas lights can also be used for the same effect.

OTHER TITLES AVAILABLE FROM BAKER'S PLAYS

OLIVER TWIST

Brian Way

18m, 3f, or as low as 5m or 3f with doubling

A straightforward version of Dickens' classic, set in 19th Century London, in which young Oliver runs away from an orphanage and is taken by the Artful Dodger to Fagin's den, where he joins in a series of adventures with Fagin's street gang until he is befriended by Mr. Brownlow. An honest, loving and exciting adaptation. For all ages.

BAKERSPLAYS.COM

OTHER TITLES AVAILABLE FROM BAKER'S PLAYS

ALICE IN AMERICA-LAND
or *Through the Picture Tube and What Alice Found There*

Dennis Snee

Comedy Fantasy / Flexible / Open Stage with Backdrops

In this fresh and lively update of Lewis Carroll's classic, Alice takes a journey through the picture tube of her family's television, and meets a mad collection of characters — with a certain difference! A White Rabbit — who lives in fear of someone's dropping "the big one." A Mock Turtle — who's a champion of consumer rights. A Dodo who's a guitarist, a Dormouse seeking political office and an Eagle who lives in the past. The Duke and Duchess have switched life roles — she's a "working duchess" while he's a "house duke." Alice herself becomes the unwitting subject for a showbiz roast with two aging, bitter comedians — the Mad Hatter and the March Hare. Through it all, Alice just wants to return home to her beloved cat. Just when it seems as though this mad world of America-land will drive her as mad as the inhabitants, she awakens, safe at home, her cat in her lap. A fanciful, biting, always funny tale of a contemporary Alice that will delight all audiences.

BAKERSPLAYS.COM